-an as in fan

Mary Elizabeth Salzmann

Consulting Editor Monica Marx, M.A./Reading Specialist

Published by SandCastle™, an imprint of ABDO Publishing Company, 4940 Viking Drive, Edina, Minnesota 55435.

Printed in the United States.

Credits
Edited by: Pam Price
Curriculum Coordinator: Nancy Tuminelly
Cover and Interior Design and Production: Mighty Media
Photo Credits: BananaStock Ltd., Comstock, Corbis Images, Hemera, Image 100, PhotoDisc, Rubberball Productions, Stockbyte

Library of Congress Cataloging-in-Publication Data

Salzmann, Mary Elizabeth, 1968-
        -An as in fan / Mary Elizabeth Salzmann.
        p. cm. -- (Word families. Set I)
        Summary: Introduces, in brief text and illustrations, the use of the letter combination "an" in such words as "fan," "pan," "man," and "plan."
        ISBN 1-59197-222-1
        1. Readers (Primary) [1. Vocabulary. 2. Reading.] I. Title.

PE1119 .S2342145 2003
428.1--dc21   2002038626

SandCastle™ books are created by a professional team of educators, reading specialists, and content developers around five essential components that include phonemic awareness, phonics, vocabulary, text comprehension, and fluency. All books are written, reviewed, and leveled for guided reading, early intervention reading, and Accelerated Reader® programs and designed for use in shared, guided, and independent reading and writing activities to support a balanced approach to literacy instruction.

Let Us Know

After reading the book, SandCastle would like you to tell us your stories about reading. What is your favorite page? Was there something hard that you needed help with? Share the ups and downs of learning to read. We want to hear from you! To get posted on the ABDO Publishing Company Web site, send us e-mail at:

sandcastle@abdopub.com

SandCastle Level: Transitional

-an Words

bran

can

fan

man

pan

van

Bran muffins and juice
make a good breakfast.

Fran waters the garden
with a watering can.

Jan has a fan in each hand.

Dan's **teacher is a** man.

Nan cooks meat and eggs in a pan.

The family will buy a
new van.

Stan Had a Plan

There once was
a boy named Stan.

Stan wanted to be
a big, strong man.

Stan's
Man Plan

So Stan came up
with a plan.

For breakfast he had
cereal with bran.

For lunch he ate
fruits and veggies
straight from the can.

Stan's dinner was steak,
fried in a pan.

Exercise was also
part of Stan's plan.

Every day he biked

and he ran.

But Stan still wasn't a man.

So Stan asked for advice
from his gran.

Gran said, "Stan, only time can make you a man."

"But while you're a boy and when you're a man, I will always be your biggest fan."

The -an Word Family

ban	man
bran	Nan
can	pan
Dan	plan
fan	ran
Fran	Stan
Gran	tan
Jan	van

Glossary

Some of the words in this list may have more
than one meaning. The meaning listed here
reflects the way the word is used in the book.

advice   an opinion given about
what someone should do

bran   the outer covering of
wheat or other grains,
often used in cereal
and muffins

cereal   a food made from grain
that you eat with milk

exercise   an activity you do to
keep your body healthy
and fit

plan   an idea about how
you are going to do
something

About SandCastle™

A professional team of educators, reading specialists, and content developers created the SandCastle™ series to support young readers as they develop reading skills and strategies and increase their general knowledge. The SandCastle™ series has four levels that correspond to early literacy development in young children. The levels are provided to help teachers and parents select the appropriate books for young readers.

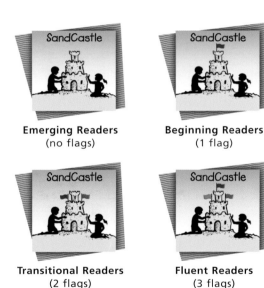

Emerging Readers
(no flags)

Beginning Readers
(1 flag)

Transitional Readers
(2 flags)

Fluent Readers
(3 flags)

These levels are meant only as a guide. All levels are subject to change.

To see a complete list of SandCastle™ books and other nonfiction titles from ABDO Publishing Company, visit **www.abdopub.com** or contact us at:

4940 Viking Drive, Edina, Minnesota 55435 • 1-800-800-1312 • fax: 1-952-831-1632